Vow-Keepers
Vow-Breakers

Simon Schrock

BIBLICAL HERITAGE SERIES No. 5

FELLOWSHIP OF CONCERNED MENNONITES
Harrisonburg, Virginia 22801

Table of Contents

With Study Helps

Dedication

George R. Brunk II

in appreciation for his faithfulness to Christ and the Scriptures . . . and his faithfulness to his ordination vows in unrelentingly proclaiming the Word of God over the years.

SIMON SCHROCK is President of Choice Books of Northern Virginia, Chairman of the Board of Directors for Choice Books Caribbean, serves on the Executive Board of the Fellowship of Concerned Mennonites, and is Pastor of Faith Christian Fellowship. He is the author of *Get on with Living, The Price of Missing Life,* and *One-Anothering.*

He, his wife Pauline, and three children live in Fairfax County, Virginia.

EARL and EMMA DELP wrote the study questions.

Preface

THERE HAS BEEN a breakdown of trust in our world. Words are no longer binding. People say one thing and then do something else. Attorneys and lawyers are being paid well to conduct law suits against those who are perceived to have broken their promises.

There was a time when a Christian's promises could basically be trusted. His words were believable. The Church taught and expected honesty and integrity. However, in recent years, things have changed. The sin of breaking promises has invaded the Church. There is little distinction between the life of the Church and the misconduct of the world on this issue.

Marriage vows are becoming meaningless and worthless. Vows that are made in the Church, before God and hundreds of witnesses, are being broken.

Ministers of the Gospel are making news headlines with their unfaithful living. Preachers who once identified certain sins and preached against them are now practicing what they preached against, and yet are considered reputable church members.

What Christians once considered sin is now the norm. What was once considered filth is now referred to as good. Clergy have been charged and taken to court for indecent exposure and sexually molesting young boys.

Is there nothing solid any more?

Can no one be trusted?

Would it not be wonderful if we could take people at their word, and believe what they say?

This book is about the sin of breaking vows and commitments. It is not a discussion of doctrinal differences, or how various denominations and congregations make their applications. These differences are not the issues I am addressing.

Since I was born and raised in the Amish Mennonite heritage, it seems proper to use illustrations from my own experience and observation. I urge the reader not to get side-tracked on where we may differ in these applications, but focus on the issue of keeping vows and promises. The Church's unfaithfulness is a sin before God, and a great hindrance to the work of the Kingdom of our Lord Jesus Christ.

Simon Schrock
February 18, 1989

ONE

God Is a Covenant Keeper

BACK IN 1972, we were building an addition to our house. We needed a plumber, so we contacted this nice man named Jesse. Jesse the plumber arrived, looked at the job, and gave us a price. We accepted the offer. The agreement was made!

But as time went on there was one catch. Jesse would not return. We called; he promised; and so it went call after call, day after day, week after week. He is on his way there today, or tomorrow, we were told again and again. The last promise we had from Jesse was that he was loading his truck to come out. That was seventeen years ago. He never did arrive, so we went ahead and did our own plumbing. Can you imagine how full Jesse's truck must be by now if he is still there loading it to come?

This story is both humorous and aggravating. The aggravation and disgust come from a promise not kept.

As I sit here writing, I experience a strange mixture of emotions within myself. On the one hand, I feel hurts, disappointments, and anger. On the other hand, I am reaching out in compassion, love, and forgiveness. Why the frustration?

Some years ago, I witnessed the marriage of a young man and woman who committed themselves to each other for the rest of their lives. He and she made a commitment to God to be loyal to each other in health or in sickness, until the day death parts them. When that vow was made to God and each other, I was among the many guests who witnessed the experience. This was a Christian church wedding, and both individuals were raised in Christian homes.

Now she is battling cancer. She is miles away from her family and friends, lying on a lonely hospital bed, hoping to recover from extensive surgery. Where is the man who promised God he would stand with her in sickness? Is he there holding her hand, assuring her she is loved? NO! The vow made to God has been broken. She is left to suffer through this without him, while he is hundreds of miles away from her, living with another woman and another commitment.

A vow has been broken! How does God view this kind of behavior?

You are "flowing with the traffic" on the interstate. Everyone is exceeding the speed limit. It seems like it must be the acceptable thing to do. Then suddenly the siren sounds behind you. You are caught! Are you guilty, or were you just flowing with the traffic? What the traffic was doing is not the question! The question is did you break the law, and are you guilty?

The flow of traffic in our culture is to break vows that were made to God and to one another. The plumber does not keep his word. The homeowner will not pay his remodeling bill. Dad never got the bike he promised his son. He never fixed the broken glass he promised his wife he would. Mom and Dad never did live within the congregation's standard of conduct as they promised God they would. The grandson is breaking his marriage vow he made to God. Our verbal vows and promises are meaningless.

This flow of vow breaking traffic is imposed upon us by our ungodly and worldly American culture. Do the disciples of Jesus flow with the traffic of their culture, or are they called to another way? Do they simply drift along with the crowd on the broad way "that leadeth to destruction," or does Jesus call them to stand up and be counted with the few on the narrow way "which leadeth unto life"?

God Is a Covenant Keeper

The congregation opened their hymn books and together they sang "On Christ the Solid Rock I Stand." They sang with the assurance of the security that Jesus Christ gives to those who obey Him. At another congregation in Washington, D.C., the believers sang together, "Christ Receiveth Sinful Men." They could sing that song from a heart of joy, because within their experience that song carried a message of hope. Men around the world sing about Jesus because He brings hope, security, and direction to their lives. They have a deep inner assurance of joy and peace because of their relationship with Jesus Christ.

Why can the Church around the world sing of their joy and assurance? Because God keeps His promises to the human race! God is a keeper of promises. He keeps His covenant with man. Therefore we have hope.

Across our land and within the Church there are hurting people who have lost hope, their security has vanished, their direction for the future is dismally blank, and they have no assurance to encourage them on. Why? It is because of broken vows and promises.

God created a people to have fellowship with Him. He made man for Himself; and for man, he made a help-meet, woman. Ah—behold, it was very good! He was pleased. Here were man and woman created to love and glorify Him.

Only a short time after God created Adam and Eve, they disobeyed God. The forbidden fruit looked lustfully good to the eye. The woman took a bite and it tasted good.

Then she handed a serving to her husband, and he also ate of the forbidden fruit. This was a deliberate act of disobedience to God, and of obedience to Satan. Now there they stood—with their glory garments vanished—shamefully, hopelessly, and sinfully naked before God. They were guilty, and the death sentence was upon them.

That death penalty has been passed on to all of humanity to this very day. The Bible states it like this, ". . . all have sinned, and come short of the glory of God." [1]

God responded to Satan with justice and promised that One would come who would ". . . bruise thy head." [2] This is a promise of hope for all people. God, in mercy, compassion, and love would send Someone to give deliverance from this curse of sin. God promised a Redeemer! Our hope depended upon God keeping His promises.

A Promise to Noah

Adam's offspring continued in their sin. "And God saw that the wickedness of man was great in the earth, and that every imagination of the thoughts of his heart was only evil continually. And it repented the Lord that he had made man on the earth, and it grieved Him in His heart." [3]

The very nature of God required Him to respond with justice to such wickedness. "And the Lord said, I will destroy man whom I have created from the face of the earth, . . ." [4]

If God destroyed man, what would happen to His promise? But God honored His promise in Noah! Speaking of Noah, the Scripture states, "But Noah found grace in the eyes of the Lord." [5] God told him, ". . . with thee will I establish my covenant." [6] God made a promise to Noah. He was obedient to God's commandments. God kept His promise, and "Noah . . . remained alive, and they that were with him in the ark." [7]

After the flood waters receded and Noah was back on

the earth, God said to Noah, "I establish my covenant with you, and with your seed after you." [8] God gave Noah the sign of a rainbow to remind him of the covenant He made. He kept His promise to Noah. To this very day the rainbow reminds us that God is a covenant keeper.

A Promise to Abram

Noah died, but God's promise to him and his descendants remained. Later, God chose a man named Abram with whom He established His covenant.

"Now the Lord had said unto Abram, Get thee out of thy country . . . unto a land that I will show thee:

"And I will make of thee a great nation, and I will bless thee, and make thy name great; and thou shalt be a blessing:

"And I will bless them that bless thee, and curse him that curseth thee: and in thee shall all families of the earth be blessed." [9] God had promised a beautiful gift to humanity. He had found a man who would carry the covenant of the promise through his generation. Read on and experience the beauty of this promise from God.

"And when Abram was ninety years old and nine, the Lord appeared to Abram and said unto him, I am the Almighty God, walk before me and be thou perfect.

"And I will make my covenant between me and thee, and will multiply thee exceedingly.

"And Abram fell on his face: and God talked with him, saying,

"As for me, behold my covenant is with thee, and thou shalt be a father of many nations.

"Neither shall thy name any more be called Abram, but thy name shall be Abraham . . . .

". . . I will establish my covenant between me and thee and thy seed after thee in their generations for an everlasting covenant . . . ." [10]

"And God said, Sarah thy wife shall bear thee a son indeed; and thou shalt call his name Isaac: and I will establish my covenant with him for an everlasting covenant, and with his seed after him." [11]

This covenant was from God. It was passed from one generation to the next, from Abraham, to Isaac, to Jacob; and handed on through history. Even though time went on, year after year, God did not forget this commitment to Abraham and all people after him.

The children of Israel were in severe bondage under the King of Egypt, and ". . . their cry came up unto God by reason of the bondage.

"And God heard their groaning, and God remembered his covenant with Abraham, with Isaac, and with Jacob.

"And God looked upon the children of Israel, and God had respect unto them." [12]

"And I have also established my covenant with them, to give them the land of Canaan,

". . . I have also heard the groaning of the children of Israel, whom the Egyptians keep in bondage; and I have remembered my covenant." [13]

God even reminded His people, "I will never break my covenant with you." [14]

God is a keeper of His covenant. He did not break His promise to the Israelites!

The Psalmist draws attention to God's fathfulness in keeping His commitments.

"He hath remembered his covenant forever, the word which he commanded to a thousand generations." [15]

"He hath given meat unto them that fear him: he will ever be mindful of his covenant.

"He sent redemption unto his people: he hath commanded his covenant forever: holy and reverend is his name." [16]

The writer of the Psalms had complete confidence that

God would keep His commitment.

Suppose God would have said, "Jacob, I simply cannot endure your unloving attitude toward me. I simply cannot stand your coldness and unkindness toward me. I cannot put up with the way you keep going away from me and keeping company with others. You children of Israel, I am done! You have broken your commitment to me over and over. I have had it with you!"

God would have had just reason to break His commitment to us sinful humans—but He did not! He loved us with an everlastng love.

As we look back through history, we notice that God's servants and prophets pleaded with Israel not to walk out on God's covenant with His people. Ezra the priest, Nehemiah, Isaiah, Jeremiah, Ezekiel, Daniel, Hosea, Zechariah, and Malachi were among those who pleaded with Israel, "Come back . . . stay with the commitment, God will fulfill it . . . the Redeemer will come."

God was indeed faithful to His promise. He kept His commitment to us by sending the Redeemer to die for our sins. He sent Jesus! Unto you is born a Saviour!
God sent Jesus Christ to live among us long enough to demonstrate by His teachings and miracles that He was indeed the promised Messiah.

After Jesus Christ suffered to pay the penalty of our sin

. . .

After they took His body from the cross and buried it

. . .

After He rose from the dead . . .

After He ascended to heaven . . .

After His Spirit came upon His followers . . .

One of them, named Peter, forcefully reminded his audience, Look Israel, the commitment is still good! It is being fulfilled! It is for you!

"Repent ye therefore, and be converted, that your sins

may be blotted out, when the times of refreshing shall come from the presence of the Lord;

"And he shall send Jesus Christ, which before was preached unto you:

". . . which God hath spoken by the mouth of all his holy prophets since the world began.

"For Moses truly said unto the fathers, A prophet shall the Lord your God raise up unto you of your brethren,

"Yea, and all the prophets from Samuel and those that follow after, as many as have spoken, have likewise foretold of these days.

"Ye are the children of the prophets, and of the covenant which God made with our fathers, saying unto Abraham, And in thy seed shall all the kindreds of the earth be blessed.

"Unto you first God, having raised up his Son Jesus, sent him to bless you, in turning away every one of you from his iniquities." [17]

Listen! What is even better, this fulfilling of the covenant is for everyone! It is good for you, too!

"Christ hath redeemed us from the curse of the law, being made a curse for us: for it is written, Cursed is every one that hangeth on a tree:

"That the blessings of Abraham might come on the Gentiles through Jesus Christ; that we might receive the promise of the Spirit through faith.

"For ye are all the children of God by faith in Christ Jesus.

"And if ye be Christ's, then are ye Abraham's seed, and heirs according to the promise." [18]

God has been faithful in keeping His promise. Therefore, ". . . Whosoever shall call upon the name of the Lord shall be saved." [19]

God did not only keep His commitment to Israel by giving them the land that flowed with milk and honey, but

He gave to all of us a better covenant. The writer of Hebrews tells us about it.

"But the ministry Jesus has received is as superior to theirs as the covenant of which he is mediator is superior to the old one, and it is founded on better promises." [20]

"For this reason Christ is the mediator of a new covenant, that those who are called may receive the promised eternal inheritance, now that he has died as a ransom to set them free from the sins committed under the first covenant."[21]

Because God gave us a superior covenant, we have a fellowship with God that makes us perfect in every good work to do His will.

"Now the God of peace that brought again from the dead our Lord Jesus, that great shepherd of the sheep, through the blood of the everlasting covenant,

"Make you perfect in every good work to do his will, working in you that which is well pleasing in his sight, through Jesus Christ, to whom be glory for ever and ever. Amen." [22]

God made a promise to all people. (Genesis 3:15) God kept it! Because He did, we have hope. That fulfilled promise we now have in Jesus Christ does not leave the believers dangling in fear and hopelessness awaiting God's judgment. Notice the closing words of the old covenant, ". . . lest I come and smite the earth with a curse."[23]

Now, take a special notice to the closing word of the new covenant, "The grace of our Lord Jesus Christ be with you all. Amen." [24]

Those last dozen words of the New Covenant explain the difference it makes to the believer whether God kept His promise or not. Instead of judgment upon us, it is God's grace.

The plumber promised, but never delivered. Men vow to each other, then violate their pledges. These broken promises leave others wounded, hurting, and bitter. Suppose God would still be "loading His truck," or just coldly have backed out of His promise to us?

God is a covenant keeper. He kept His promise to us. Because of God's unfailing faithfulness, we can depend assuredly on His grace in life or death.

Since God is a covenant keeper, do you think He expects less of His blood-bought saints?

[1] Romans 3:23.
[2] Genesis 3:15.
[3] Genesis 6:5-6.
[4] Genesis 6:7a.
[5] Genesis 6:8.
[6] Genesis 6:18a.
[7] Genesis 7:23.
[8] Genesis 9:9.
[9] Genesis 12:1-3.
[10] see Genesis 17:1-7.
[11] Genesis 17:19.
[12] Exodus 2:23-24.
[13] Exodus 6:4-5.
[14] Judges 2:1.
[15] Psalm 105:8.
[16] Psalm 111:5, 9.
[17] Acts 3:19-26.
[18] Galatians 3:13-14, 26-29.
[19] Romans 10:13.
[20] Hebrews 8:6 N.I.V.
[21] Hebrews 9:15 N.I.V.
[22] Hebrews 13:20-21.
[23] Malachi 4:6.
[24] Revelation 22:21.

Questions for Discussion

1. How many covenants did God make with the human family? What was the nature of each?
2. Distinguish between a covenant, a vow, a promise.
3. What is the difference between the close of the Old Covenant (Testament) and the close of the New?
4. What are some of the results of unkept vows and commitments?
5. Did anyone ever break a commitment made to you? What did it do to you?
6. What makes a vow binding?

TWO

Humanity Benefits

HOW ARE OUR lives affected since God faithfully fulfilled His covenant with us? What does the keeping of commitments mean to us today? What does it mean to others when you keep your commitments?

Hope

First, the keeping of commitments means hope. Elizabeth and Zacharias became parents of a promised son, whom they named John. The birth of this son brought on a new vigor of hope. His father praised God and was ". . . filled with the Holy Ghost, and prophesied, saying,

"Blessed be the Lord God of Israel; for he hath visited and redeemed his people,

"And hath raised up an horn of salvation for us in the house of his servant David;

"As he spake by the mouth of his holy prophets, which have been since the world began:

"That we should be saved from our enemies, and from the hand of all that hate us;

"To perform the mercy promised to our fathers, and to remember his holy covenant;

"the oath which he sware to our father Abraham." [25]

God remembered His holy covenant (commitment) to Abraham. Zacharias knew that the birth of their son John was a promise fulfilled and that the Redeemer would soon be here. That was real hope fulfilled.

The keeping of commitments means hope. There is a commitment of loyalty that goes with becoming a member of the Church. What hope is there for the future of a congregation if members make verbal expressions of loyalty, but in reality they do not observe the understood practices and behavior of the Church? What hope is there if members are only present for half or less of the church services and meetings? What hope is there for the future if the members choose selective attendance, and instead give their loyalty to whatever sports team may be kicking or throwing a ball around in a city stadium? What hope is there if members deliberately choose worldly entertainment over worshipping with the fellow-believers of the Church? How many church meetings can you miss and still live in the context of your commitment? How many of the Church's positions can one "overlook" without being disloyal? What will be the future condition of a Church with 200 members when only a faithful thirty attend the Sunday evening service?

Suppose God would have not kept His promise to send us Jesus? Our future would be hopeless. But He kept His promise. That is hope.

Disloyalty to one's commitment results in hopelessness. Loyalty gives an anticipation of hope for the future. Keeping promises establishes hope.

Security

The second blessing of keeping commitments is security. Noah experienced a security and safety with his family that no other person on the entire earth enjoyed. Rain began to fall for the first time in history when Noah and his family were secure inside the ark of safety.

"By faith Noah, being warned of God of things not seen as yet, moved with fear, prepared an ark to the saving of his house; by which he condemned the world, and became heir of the righteousness which is by faith." [26] Noah was secure inside. Commitments that are kept bring security.

Whenever a husband or wife must be concerned whether the other will be true to their marriage vows, there is insecurity and fear. A suspicious eye must be kept on each other. This puts a strain on ther relationship.

Can you imagine the deep down suspicious insecurity of the pastors' wives whose husbands counsel other women, advising them that under certain circumstances divorce is an option? If that is his advice to others, it must certainly be an option for himself. Therefore, we have insecure leaders attempting to give security and guidance to others. Vows, commitments, and covenants are meant for security. When they are broken, it brings insecurity to others. When they are kept, it brings security to yourself and others. Noah, for example, landed safe and dry because God was faithful to His commitment.

Direction

The third blessing of keeping commitments is that it gives you a sense of direction. You will not be swept off course by every little breeze of new sounding doctrine.

Abraham was a covenant keeper. He had a sense of direction for his life.

"By faith Abraham, when he was called to go out into a place which he should after receive for an inheritance, obeyed; and he went out, not knowing where he went.

"By faith he sojourned in the land of promise, as in a strange country, dwelling in tabernacles with Isaac and Jacob, the heirs with him of the same promise:

"For he looked for a city which hath foundations, whose builder and maker is God." [27]

"These all died in faith, not having received the promises, but having seen them afar off, and were persuaded of them, and embraced them and confessed that they were strangers and pilgrims on the earth." [28]

"But now they desire a better country, that is, an heavenly: wherefore God is not ashamed to be called their God: for he hath prepared for them a city." [29]

We can see in the book of Hebrews that Abraham did not have his heart on possessions and real estate here on the earth. His heart was fixed on the covenant between him and God. Therefore, this gave him a long range perception of where he was going. He was so far-sighted he overlooked the pleasures of his present age, and aimed for a heavenly city where "God is not ashamed to be called their God." His commitment gave him direction to a city that hath foundations laid by God, where he would enjoy himself with his Maker for all eternity.

When a person makes a commitment to Jesus Christ and His Church, it is then within that honest commitment that one has a new sense of direction. A commitment to Jesus Christ gives you direction. It gives you a reference point. It gives you a home base.

In the difficulties of life, Jesus and the Church to whom you are committed become the reference point for your life. When there are tough decisions to be made, when the pressures of the world press in on you, when disappointments and sorrow sweep over you, there is a home base, it is Jesus and His Church.

My friend's life was shattered to find that his wife had actually left him. They had both been church members, but his commitment to Jesus and the Church was very shallow. He did not have a clear sense of direction for his life like Abraham did. With an empty house and no direction, he turned to Jesus Christ, and made a sincere commitment to follow Him. Even in the absence of his wife, he now finds a sense of direction in his relationship with Jesus Christ and the supporting believers in the Church.

Abraham had a keen sense of direction. It was because of his loyalty to his commitment.

Assurance

The fourth blessing of keeping commitments is assurance. What is more comforting than knowing you can rely on God's Word and His promises? What is more comforting than a quiet inner assurance that all is well between you and your Creator?

Simeon was a righteous and devout man in Jerusalem, who was waiting for the promised Messiah to come. The Holy Spirit revealed to him that he would see Jesus before he died. Simeon was moved by the Spirit to go into the courts of the temple. There he met the parents of Jesus, who brought Him to the temple to do for Him what the law required. Simeon took Jesus up in his arms, blessed God, and said, "Lord, now lettest thou thy servant depart in peace, according to thy word:

"For mine eyes have seen thy salvation, Which thou hast prepared before the face of all people; A light to lighten the Gentiles, and the glory of thy people Israel." [30]

God kept His promise to Simeon. Therefore, He reached out and picked up the child Jesus, and with a flooding of inner assurance, he praised God, and was ready to die. Because God kept His commitment and sent us Jesus, we too can have that joyful, inner assurance. The Spirit moved John to write an Epistle (I John) in order that our joy may be full.

According to the Scriptures, "These things have I written unto you that believe on the name of the Son of God; that ye may know that ye have eternal life, and that ye may believe on the name of the Son of God." [31]

Because of God's covenant with us, today we can live in joy and with the assurance that if the world is destroyed tomorrow, we will be safe in the presence of Jesus.

Just as God's keeping of His covenant gives us assurance, so will our keeping of commitments give others assurance of our integrity and trustworthiness to others. When we break our commitments, we destroy others' confidence in our integrity and honesty. God gave us assurance of His trustworthiness. We owe the same to others.

David and Jonathan made a friendship commitment. They renewed their commitment to each other as the pressure of life increased. Later they made a commitment before God. Do you know what that did for them? Jonathan went to David "and strengthened his hand in God." Their commitments to each other gave them hope, security, direction, and assurance.[32]

Edward Dayton wrote, "To be human is to long for commitments from others. Commitment is at the foundations of all human relationships. To put it another way, commitment is what human relationships are all about. The person who withdraws all commitment to others ceases to be human." [33]

Commitments are to give us hope, security, direction, and assurance. God has kept His commitment. Therefore, we have these blessings.

If God had not kept His promise to us, we would not have the assurance of God's unfailing faithfulness.

What does this mean to us? God set an example for us. He is the model of what commitment keeping means and the benefits it imparts to people. His Spirit-filled believers are expcected to keep their commitments. To do less is to dishonor God.

[25] Luke 1:67-73.
[26] Hebrews 11:7.
[27] Hebrews 11:8-10.
[28] Hebrews 11:13.
[29] Hebrews 11:16.
[30] Luke 2:29-32.
[31] See 1 John 1:4; 5:13.
[32] See 1 Sam. 18:3; 20:11-12; 23:16-18a.
[33] *Whatever Happened to Commitment*, Edward Dayton, Zondervan.

Questions for Discussion

1. Name some of the benefits of kept vows.
2. Should vows ever be conditional? Why or why not?
3. What would be the results if God did not keep His promises?
4. Give some examples of man's failure to keep his commitments to God, as found in the Bible. What were the results?
5. Does one's commitment to Christ affect others? How?
6. Try to imagine a world in which most people failed to keep their commitments.

THREE

It Depends

"SHE WAS PRETTY. Her smile and twinkle in her eye extended a welcome that felt good. I was seated with three business associates in a secluded corner of an elegant restaurant in a fine Houston hotel.

"She and another beautiful young woman had taken a seat at the table near ours. As she sat down, she brushed against my arm, and then apologized warmly. Her touch, her voice, and her smile made me turn and almost forget why I was there. Her body language and smile shouted an invitation. I was tempted." That was Wilmer's testimony.

Wilmer was a young businessman traveling for his company to all the major cities in the United States and Canada, and some places overseas. He was successful, and his bosses were well pleased. He was given an unlimited expense account, free membership in the country club, and all the fringe benefits any company offered. His work took him away from home almost every week. The sales trips were hard work. He tried to make at least three sales calls per day, and that meant traveling to at least three different cities each day.

He had come to Houston on a Friday evening. The night before in Atlanta, he received a call from his immediate supervisor, the vice president of marketing. He was told the president of a large automotive parts company was ready to sign the contract he had delivered to him two weeks earlier. His boss had arranged for him and the president of the auto parts store to meet Friday evening at a hotel in Houston.

Here is Wilmer's testimony of what happened that night in Houston. "I had called on customers in Boston, New York, Newark, Greensboro, and Atlanta. I was weary, and wanted nothing more than to go home. But after the boss' call, I changed my flight and called my family to tell them I would be a day late. They did not like it because their weekend plans had to be changed. I was tired and weary, and felt like my boss had taken advantage of me.

"So when I came into the hotel in Houston, I rushed to my room to clean up and prepare for the meeting. I barely got ready for the dinner meeting on time. I was exhausted and a bit angry—and then she smiled at me. The invitation was there. I knew all the signs: the body language, the seductive attire, the soft touch. I had seen it often while traveling with my business peers. Many of them looked for female companions to spend the night with. Their wives and families would never know; or so they thought. But then they were never quite sure.

"By the time dinner was over and the contract signed, I knew that the chance of brushing my arm had been no accident. The president of the company was so pleased with my work he had arranged a 'tip' for me. He wanted to show his appreciation for my good work."[34]

Wilmer had the offer before him. Would he accept?

Purpose and Value of Commitments

Commitments, covenants, vows, and promises have a purpose. They are of extreme importance and value to humanity. The Psalmist helps us gain some important insights on the subject. He asks, "Lord, who may dwell in your sanctuary? Who may live on your holy hill?" The answer; "He whose walk is blameless and who does what is righteous, who speaks the truth from his heart and has no slander on his tongue, who does his neighbor no wrong and casts no slur on his fellow man, who despises a vile man but honors those who fear the Lord, who *keeps his oath even when it hurts.*" [35]

Notice the Psalmist's point on keeping his oath. Who may live in God's holy hill? The oath keepers! Then in the closing part of the Psalm he says, "He who does these things will never be shaken." [36] What is the value of being vow keepers? It keeps you from being shaken by every wind of doctrine, seducing spirits, and doctrines of devils that may lead to departing from the faith.[37]

In Psalm 116, the Psalmist again addresses the issue of vow keeping. In verses 1 through 11, he draws attention to God's goodness and blessings to us. The Lord heard his voice and cry for mercy. "The cords of death entangled me, . . . I was overcome by trouble and sorrow . . . then I called on the Name of the Lord . . . The Lord is gracious and righteous . . . full of compassion. For you, O Lord, have delivered my soul from death, my eyes from tears, my feet from stumbling." [38]

Look at all the blessings from God! Then the Psalmist asks, "How can I repay the Lord for all his goodness to me?" [39]

Here is how! "I will lift up the cup of salvation and call on the name of the Lord." Now be sure and get the second thing he mentions. "I will fulfill my vows to the Lord in the presence of all his people." [40]

David emphasizes the important principle of fulfilling his vows in the presence of the people. Jesus' teachings affirmed the importance of a public commitment. He said, "Whosoever therefore shall confess me before men, him will I confess also before my Father which is in heaven. But whosoever shall deny me before men, him will I also deny before my Father which is in heaven." [41]

A public commitment made to Jesus Christ establishes

a reference point, and a home base for living. Life's many decisions are made in response to that commitment. Making and living out a commitment to Jesus Christ publicly is a must to be part of the kingdom of God.

David, after saying, I will fulfill my vow to the Lord, sees hope and assurance for eternity. "Precious in the sight of the Lord is the death of his saints." [42]

Notice the progression here. Give thanks to God for His goodness. How can I repay God for all this? By keeping vows to God in the presence of the people. And then for the vow keepers, death is precious in the sight of the Lord.

Here the Psalmist gives us a sandwich. The meat is the saints' death. In verse 14, the slice of bread is the vows kept before God and man. In verse 15, he lays on the good news about the death of his vow keeping saints. Then in verse 18, he tops it off with vows fulfilled to the Lord and humanity. It is the kept vows that make it a precious sandwich. Because of his loyalty to God, he can say death is precious.

How will vow breakers face death? Is a vow breaker ready for death? Or would it be more appropriate to ask if he is ready for life, and knows how to live?

Vows Are To Hold You

God commanded the people of Israel to keep their vows. "This is what the Lord commands: When a man makes a vow to the Lord or takes an oath to obligate himself by a pledge, he must not break his word but must do everything he said." [43]

God expects that when a vow or commitment is made, it is actually fulfilled as promised. That means to *do* according to *all* that proceeds out of your mouth. This, therefore, helps you who made the vow to do what is right, regardless of whether you feel like it or not. It holds a person on the right track.

The Psalmist instructs us to ". . . fulfill your vows to the most high." [44] A vow or commitment made to each other is really a vow to God. Our actions, attitudes, and the way we treat each other is really the way we treat God. If we are disloyal in our commitments to each other, we are really disloyal to God. If we can establish in our hearts that the way we fulfill our commitments to each other is really how we fulfill our vows to the Most High, it will help us to establish loyalty and respect in our commitments to each other. Jesus said, ". . . Inasmuch as ye have done it unto the least of these my brethren, ye have done it unto me." [45]

Vows Are To Be Taken Seriously

Wise Solomon wrote, "It is a trap for a man to dedicate something rashly and only later to consider his vows." [46]

"Do not be quick with your mouth, do not be hasty in your heart to utter anything before God, God is in heaven and you are on earth, so let your words be few. . . . When you make a vow to God, do not delay in fulfilling it. He has no pleasure in fools; fulfill your vow. It is better not to vow than to make a vow and not fulfill it." [47]

Following Jesus is a serious commitment, and is to be entered into with all sincerity. Jesus' teaching emphasizes this. He told the multitudes that were following Him that "whosoever doth not bear his cross, and come after me, cannot be my disciple." Then He gave an illustration. "For which of you, intending to build a tower, sitteth not down first and counteth the cost, whether he have sufficient to finish it? Lest haply, after he hath laid the foundation, and is not able to finish it, all that behold it begin to mock him, Saying, This man began to build and was not able to finish. So likewise, whosoever he be of you that forsaketh not all that he hath, he cannot be my disciple." [48]

A serious commitment, where one has resolved from the heart to pay the price of discipleship, will hold that person solid in their faith. That commitment will help keep the eye on the goal. It will be very helpful in weathering the stormy onslaught of the Devil. Keeping true to a commitment to Jesus Christ will carry you through.

In the early 1970's, the charismatic movement struck in many Christian communities. It divided believers into different camps of thought within local congregations. Eventually, it led to divisions within families, and among close brothers and sisters in the Lord. The aftermath left leaders and parents with emotional pain and many disappointments. However, some families survived without division. They were the ones who remained loyal to their commitment to their Church, and who did not rebel or belittle the Lord's anointed. It was those families and their children that made it through the storm with their faith strengthened.

On the other hand, those who wavered from their commitments of loyalty and challenged the Lord's chosen leaders in unscriptural ways were the ones whose families shipwrecked and the pieces floated in all directions. The casualties today are scattered in many places.

We do recognize there are those who discussed and reasoned doctrinal differences with the local Church and her leaders. When the differences proved to be irreconcilable, they chose in a Christian manner to make their commitment to another fellowship.

Edward Dayton wrote: "Commitment is at the foundation of all human relationships . . . To be human is to long for commitments from others." [47]

Commitments and promises mean dependability. They mean we can count on each other to keep the Faith, and to maintain sound doctrine. We can count on someone to help put our pieces back together when our world falls apart. When we hurt and have needs, commitment means someone will be there to help and support us.

Commitment means we can call a friend at 2:00 a.m., and he will not hang up on us. It means we know the pastor will listen or come when we call. The police and the fire department will respond to a scream of terror in the night. Commitment means the green slips of paper are worth what the figures say—that is if the commitments are kept. Our government is committed to redeem them at face value. If the government tomorrow at 10:00 a.m. withdrew their commitment to redeem your money, we would be in serious trouble. Suppose your ten dollars would be redeemed in proportion to how you keep your commitments and promises. Would your money be worth twenty, thirty, fifty, or one hundred percent?

"Commitment is what human relationships are all about. For we are made to live in relationships with others. The person who withdraws all commitments to others ceases to be human." [50] And for certain, he ceases to be spiritual. Commitments are for our good. When they are taken seriously, they will guide us through life's storms and battles.

Commitment is Costly

Commitment has a price tag. It is not what you would call a pleasure trip of relaxation and enjoyment. However, it does bring joy and fulfillment. It requires giving of ourselves, our time and energy, our resources and thoughts, and "even our very soul. And because of its cost, we admire it in others and fear it for ourselves." [51]

It has risks that make it even more costly. It means we give ourselves to others, and they may still turn away. Then we are left to suffer rejection and hurts as we realize their commitment to us was not the same as ours to them. This can be very costly.

It was so for Sarah. She was committed to being loyal to her husband until death severed their marriage bond.

Her husband's commitment was not that deep and loyal. He was sidetracked from his vow as he gave attention to other women and their horses. Sarah spent long days and nights waiting and praying for her husband to return to his commitment to her. Her dedication cost her a high price of pain and disappointment. However, her loyalty and faithfulness was rewarded when her husband returned and they were united again through reconciliation and forgiveness. Today this couple enjoys a beautiful relationship because one was willing to pay the high price of commitment. Both of them are stronger in their Christian faith than before.

When we commit ourselves to others and to causes on behalf of others, we are no longer our own. We put ourselves on the availability list to be called upon for help we may not be prepared or even able to give.

The highest and costliest commitment ever made was the one God made to humanity. He promised to send us His Son to redeem us from the curse and penalty of sin. The price of this commitment can be seen in the life and death of God's only Son Jesus Christ. The Bible says, "For he hath made him to be sin for us, who knew no sin; that we might be made the righteousness of God in him." [52] Because of God's commitment to us, He sent Jesus to fulfill the promise He made to all people. (See Genesis 3:15.) The price of fulfilling that promise meant that He became the sin offering on our behalf, even though we did not desire such an act of mercy.

In relation to God's commitment to us, Edward Dayton points out what our response ought to be. "On the basis of His commitment to us, God calls us to be committed to Him." [53] God's Word says, "What? know ye not that your body is the temple of the Holy Ghost which is in you, which ye have of God, and ye are not your own? For ye are bought with a price: therefore glorify God in your body, and in your spirit, which are God's." [54] To glorify God in our body means a resolute commitment of loyalty to Jesus Christ and His Church. As Dayton wrote, "This is total commitment, for it involves all of life. It is a transfer of allegiance from one kingdom to another. We can say with Paul that 'once we were ... but now we are ...' Total commitment to God, the One who is for us, can be made without fear of rejection, for there is no turning away in His personality. He will never leave us nor forsake us." [55]

Dayton points out another dimension of Christian commitment that our personal egos find very difficult to accept. It is the reality that a commitment to God means a commitment to His Church. He says, "Not only are we no longer our own, neither are we committed only to God; we are also fitted into the body, the Church. We are part of one another, and the measure of our commitment to God is our commitment to one another." [56] "If a man say, I love God, and hateth his brother, he is a liar: for he that loveth not his brother whom he hath seen, how can he love God whom he hath not seen?" [57] A commitment to God and the Church means we no longer selfishly seek what we want for ourselves, but we seek what is best for the body of believers. We are called from self-indulgence, worldly ambitions, and a drive for personal gain, to serving God and others.

"When James Calvert went out as a missionary to the cannibals of the Fiji Islands, the captain of the ship sought to turn him back. 'You will lose your life and the lives of those with you if you go among such savages!', he cried. Calvert only replied, 'We died before we came here.' " [58]

The depth of this commitment brought a willingness to die for the sake of others. Rarely do we find this depth of commitment among us. All too few are committed to live for the sake of others, let alone die for them.

Allan Lee Stoltzfus died of cancer at the age of 52. His

life was committed to Jesus Christ and the good of others. The principle of his life was that people were more important than things. Bishop Jonathan Stoltzfus stated Allan's life principal in the memorial message, "The principle of brotherly love is more important than the principle of self-interest." He was deeply committed to this principle. His life of concern and caring brought a healing touch to many people. His commitment was beyond ambitions and possessions for himself. The large crowd of people who attended the memorial service was in itself an affirmation that his deep commitment to others was a blessing to many. Too many of us are not committed to anything greater than or beyond ourselves. Allen was committed to a cause greater than himself. Therefore, even though death has taken him from us, he lives on.

Are commitments important? Katie Wiebe wrote in the *Gospel Herald*, "Promises are important, because society looks down when people don't keep them." [59]

John Haggai wrote, "Integrity is carrying out a commitment after the environment in which the commitment was made has dissipated." [60] This means being true to all commitments after the excitement and newness has worn off and the honeymoon period is over.

What happens when commitments are kept? "A used lumber dealer in Kitchener, Ontario . . . always rejoiced when he saw any kind of Mennonite walk in the door. 'Mennonites always pay their bills,' he commented. He didn't worry about the debts they incurred with him." [61]

What happened to Wilmer? Did he accept the offer, or was there something that carried him through the storm? "I sat on the bed and cried. Why hadn't somebody told me about these traps? No one in the Christian college I attended even hinted about the social ethics of business. If any of my professors even knew of these things, they certainly did not discuss them with their students. No one at Colorado University helped me either. As a matter of fact, the opposite was true.

"As I sat there shaking on my hotel bed I thanked my Lord for preserving me again. I made a decision to do all I could to help other Christian business people avoid damaging social practices that were so flagrant and so tempting.

"There on the hotel bed the word hit me. Commitment! I had made a commitment to my wife. I'd promised to be ever true to her. Her alone. A commitment that I did not want to break, a commitment I could not break.

"The commitment went further than family. I was a child of the King. I had committed my life to King Jesus. He had plans for me and my life would count for him. His directive was to flee from the lusts of the flesh. I couldn't break that commitment.

"My training in school and the examples I saw around me in society certainly did not teach commitment. Just the contrary. By word and example I was taught to be loyal to myself and to use every means to promote self. Let other persons fend for themselves. I was taught to center all activity on myself and become independent and wealthy so I could take care of myself and my family and indulge in whatever money can buy. If you can afford it, it must be right, society told me. These were the things I learned in school.

"But my parents and my church back in Henderson, Nebraska, had sneaked something else into my life. It lay dormant there in the dark recesses of my mind for many years. Until I began to face those awful temptations during those wearying sales trips.

"Then there was that 'something' that kept me from yielding to those temptations. It may have been the memory of my dad's voice. He taught me much by his story telling. 'This is how it was in the Old Country,' he would say. And by the time he had recounted some anecdote that usually had us rolling on the floor with laughter, he had taught those basic truths I so sorely needed later on. My parents instilled one unshakable truth and that is commitment.

"Commitment meant many things. 'You belong to this family, and we do things this way.' 'A member of the Church never needs to sign a contract, his word is good.' 'No neighbor ever needs to go to bed hungry if there is food in our house, we always share.' 'We never buy things for ourselves if we owe someone else money.'

" 'Why do we do these things?' I asked. 'Because we are committed to Christ and He taught us to live this way!' This made sense to me as a child and even later on when I saw my business peers violating all those basic truths. 'We are committed to Christ . . .'

"That was the basic foundation. What it all meant escaped me for the most part. I'm not sure I fully understand it now. But I understood since my youth that to be committed to Christ, to family and to the Church stood in direct contrast to selfishness. To be true to the basic teaching of my family, my Church and God's Word meant that my life, as important as it may be, must always be subservient to Christ and to my Christian brothers and sisters.

"When this became clear to me I could face the temptations of the business world. The wiles of a beautiful young woman who tried to take advantage of a lonely businessman posed no lasting problem to me. But I could also understand the difficulties many of my Christian friends experienced when they yielded to the common problems of the day.

"When our Lord taught us to submit ourselves one to another, he was giving us a key to freedom very few people ever learn. When we make a commitment to a cause, to an organization, to a friend, to a loved one, we can relax and enjoy that relationship to the fullest.

"I did not learn to be committed to a cause in college. If my father and mother and my Sunday school teachers had not sneaked it into my life when they did, I would have been a spiritual casualty during those hectic, busy days of travel and business.

"Let's make a new commitment. Let's rededicate ourselves to a single-minded service to our Lord, to our familes, to our Church and to our conferences. I suggest we would have far fewer spiritual casualties.

" 'My son, keep my words, and treasure my commandments within you. Keep my commandments and live, and my teaching as the apple of your eye. Bind them to your fingers; write them on the tablet of your heart. Say to wisdom, 'You are my sister,' and call understanding your intimate friend; that they may keep you from an adulteress, from the foreigner who flatters with her words.' (Proverbs 7:1-5)." [62]

[32] See 1 Sam. 18:3; 20:11-12; 23:16-18a.
[33] *Whatever Happened to Commitment,* Edward Dayton, Zondervan.
[34] *The Market Place,* Nov.-Dec. 1986.
[35] See Psalm 15:1-4 N.I.V.
[36] Psalm 15:5b N.I.V.
[37] See Eph. 4:14, 2 Tim. 4:1.
[38] See Psalm 116:1-8 N.I.V.
[39] Psalm 116:12 N.I.V.
[40] Psalm 116:18.
[41] Matthew 10:32-33.
[42] Psalm 116:15.
[43] See Numbers 30:1-2 N.I.V.
[44] Psalm 50:14b N.I.V.
[45] Matthew 25:40.
[46] Proverbs 20:25 N.I.V.
[47] Ecclesiastes 5:2, 4-5.
[48] Luke 14:27-30, 33.
[49] Edward Dayton, *Whatever Happened to Commitment,* Zondervan.

[50] Edward Dayton, *Whatever Happened to Commitment,* Zondervan.
[51] *Ibid.*
[52] 2 Corinthians 5:21.
[53] Edward Dayton, *Whatever Happened to Commitment,* Zondervan.
[54] I Corinthians 6:19-20.
[55] Edward Dayton, *Whatever Happened to Commitment,* Zondervan.
[56] Edward Dayton, *Whatever Happened to Commitment,* Zondervan.
[57] 1 John 4:20.
[58] David Augsburger, *Living Quotations,* Bethany Publishers, Minneapolis, MN.
[59] Katie Wiebe, *The Gospel Herald,* 11-18-86.
[60] John Haggai, *How to Win Over Loneliness,* Jeremy Books, Minneapolis, MN.
[61] Katie Wiebe, *Gospel Herald,* 11-18-86.
[62] *The Market Place,* Nov.-Dec., 1986.

Questions for Discussion

1. Should one ever break a vow or commitment? Why or why not?

2. Why make commitments? What is their purpose and value?

3. What is the cost of making a vow? Of breaking one?

4. What needs to be taken into consideration before one makes a vow?

5. When does the keeping of a vow become costly? Is the cost ever too high?

6. What should parents do in preparing their children for life's commitments?

FOUR

When Vows Aren't Kept

GOD MADE A COMMITMENT to the people He created!

I'll send you a Saviour!

God called a special people to watch, to wait, to expect His promise to be fulfilled. Israel was that tribe of people. They did not always keep their part of the covenant.

But God was faithful! Unto us a child was born, unto us a Son was given. Unto us was born in the city of David a Saviour, which is Christ the Lord. Therefore we have hope, security, direction for our lives, and assurance for the future.

That is the way commitments kept will work for you. Commitments kept will guide you through life's storm. That is what kept Wilmer in a time of severe temptation and testing. On the other hand, what happens when vows are not kept?

Broken Marriage Vows

A marriage vow is a vow to God. It is a vow to your spouse, to those attending the ceremony, and to the whole world. It is a vow that you will accept your responsibility in marriage, you will be loyal, you will be a helper and a partner until the day either of you will have taken your last breath. A vow in marriage means you will be loyal to your partner and be a companion even through the experience of death. It means you will stick with your spouse when your spouse needs you most.

Taking such a vow is a serious step in life. It may not be taken lightly. Shouldn't anyone taking such a step prepare, educate, and commit himself or herself for the task?

What would you do if your teenage son would slide into the cockpit of a six passenger airplane and announce that he is going to "take it for a spin," and invite you to go along? Bear in mind, he has had no flight training and no prior instruction from an experienced pilot. Would you slide in and say let's chance it? Or would you say, "Wait a minute, what do you know about airplanes?" If he responded with, "I think I can handle it," would you give in? When I get on an airplane, I like to at least have the impression that the pilot has had prior instructions and understands the risks and responsibilities of being a pilot.

Taking a marriage vow is more serious than flying an airplane. Flying an airplane requires hours and hours of instruction. Shouldn't a vow in marriage be taken with equal seriousness?

In airplane crashes, people are physically killed. When vows are broken, people are emotionally crippled for life.

What is happening with marriage vows in our present North American culture? A friend told of going to his high school class reunion, where former students met who had not seen each other for years. The atmosphere there indicated that living with the same partner for twenty years was unusual. The discussions between old time friends was about their marriage, divorces, remarriages, and how many marriage partners each had had. My friend was loyal to his marriage vow. He and his wife were still living together, and enjoying their first marriage. This prompted remarks of surprise and almost disbelief. "You're still living with the same wife?" he was asked, as though he was a misfit in society.

You likely already know the statistics of American marriages. You probably heard it again and again—one out of two will end in separation and dissolution. David A. Seamands asks a frightening question, "Do you realize that the United States is responsible for one-half of the reported divorces in the entire world?" That does not include the broken, fractured, and separated marriages that are not statistics. Neither does it include those who are emotionally and spiritually divorced, and yet existing under the same roof. Seamands reminds us, "Evangelical Christians are not exempt, and are being added to the divorce statistics at an alarming rate." [63]

With all the advancements of technology, the time savers, the luxuries, the automatics, the instants, the "do it for you" gadgets, and all the "computerized stuff" we have in our homes, things ought to be getting better. We should have more time left over to enjoy our marriages and home life. There should be time to give stability to our marriage commitments. But the situation is getting worse and worse.

"Sociologists now estimate that between 25 and 50 million children will be raised by one parent because of divorce during the first eighteen years of their life." [64]

How Does This Affect the Children?

It is devastating! Erik is a young boy who is often seen riding his bicycle around in the suburban community where he lives. If he finds children playing in a yard somewhere, he may stop and spend the day with them. If my son is outside when he rides by, he may choose to stay for a long visit. Sometimes he rides his bicycle on a dangerous and busy highway a long way from home. Erik lives in the house his dad comes to after work. His parents are divorced, and he is left alone to survive for himself and wander aimlessly throughout the community. Erik is not an isolated case. Because of broken marriage vows, millions of children are left to wander aimlessly into adulthood.

An article in *The Washington Post* addressed the subject of "How Divorce Affects Children." The journalist pointed to some alarming facts. Here are some of their findings.

"When you consider that each year since 1972 more than a million children have been in families that divorced, it makes sense for the Select Committee on Children, Youth, and Families to take a look at the impact of divorce on children.

"Dr. Gene H. Brody, co-director of the program for the Study of Competence in Children and Families, and a professor in the Department of Child and Family Development at the University of Georgia testified that behavioral scientists are beginning to examine 'the interplay among the stresses experienced by members of single parent households.'

"The way parents behaved after divorce toward each other and their children had much more effect on the children's development than the divorce itself.

"Some children exhibit severe or sustained disruptions in developments, . . . the negative effects of divorce are not inevitable."

He cited research on middle class preschoolers that showed that divorce often results in disorganized households. Children had less frequent meals with their mothers, irregular bed times, and arrived late at school. "Furthermore," he testified, "divorce was followed by a breakdown in the mother's use of appropriate and consistent discipline, fewer demands for mature and independent behavior from the child, and less parent-child communication."

"Significantly, it was primarily in those families in which household organization was disrupted, and in which the quality of parenting was severely undermined by the stress of the divorce, that children displayed more behavior problems ... which were associated with declines in intellectual abilities and social relationships over a two year period."

Dr. Judith S. Wallerstein testified "that a study of 113 mainly white middle class children, who were 3 to 18 at the time of separation, shows that many weathered the breakdown but a significant number continue to suffer the effects of divorce a full decade after the marital rupture.

"By 1984, more than 9 million children lived with divorced or separated parents. Their numbers have become so substantial that even if a small portion are living with depressed, stressed out, combative parents, it is a significant group of young people." [65]

Is there any wonder that we have a society of law breaking young people? Surely there must be some connection with vow breaking parents and a violent, murderous, suicidal generation of young people! What will this culture be like when these nine million children become the political, civic, and business leaders of our communities?

To put it mildly, broken marriage vows are devastating to children who are the helpless victims.

How Does It Affect Spouses?

"My mind is filled with fear and doubt and distrust and hopelessness. I do not want to live any longer." [66]

So wrote Elizabeth Lapp after she learned she was no longer the only woman in her husband's life. Unkept vows, divorce or no divorce, inflict deep wounds, severe depression, extreme stress, feelings of alienation, and cause a totally gloomy future. Deep hurts and tears mixed with anger, resentment, bitterness, and disappointments are the results of broken vows. It is a disruption of God's design for marriage.

For some of the victims of broken marriages, it would be easier to accept the death of a spouse than the trauma of unkept vows. They could at least think back and remember the pleasant and meaningful times together and get some comfort and encouragement by singing "Precious Memories."

A lady was looking for a book on marriage. I referred to a certain book with the comment that the author was weak on divorce. She did not want that book for her husband. The fact that broken vows and divorce have become so acceptable today brings feelings of insecurity and fear to marriages. The pastor who counsels that divorce and remarriage are acceptable in certain situations is giving his own partner a signal of insecurity. His wife may wonder if her husband will find some reason to divorce her and marry someone who "understands" him.

Broken vows and divorce not only break marriages, they break people. Marriages are like plywood bonded together with strong bonding glue. To get it apart, you must tear it apart. The wood breaks and splinters apart rather than separating at the glue joints. Severing marriage relationships tears persons apart, and inflicts deep emotional pain. It is a sin against God.

How Does It Affect the Larger Family?

The behavior of the unsaved world is wickedness and evil in the sight of God. He sent the fire of judgment and destruction on Sodom for its wickedness. How long will He withhold judgment from our land? A person could take a bit of comfort by thinking this evil is in the outside world, and God will surely spare judgment for the sake of the Church. However, what is happening in the Church is a shame and a disgrace to God Himself.

The Mennonite Church was once known for its low divorce rate. Tragically, that has changed. Grandparents and parents are grieving and hurting because of what has happened to their children and grandchildren. From bleeding and disappointed hearts, their stories are told over and over again. They share the hurts and grief of having to live with the fact that their own children and grandchildren have divorced and remarried.

At Christmas time families have their get togethers. Their children come home with "another partner." They broke vows with the first one, and now are introducing the family to another person in their lives. In many situations, Mom and Dad are grieved and heart-broken. There they sit, in their favorite chairs in the living room, remembering the wedding, the help they gave, the beauty of the vows, and the potentially bright future. They remember accepting and welcoming the new in-law into the family. They remember how they loved them and were excited about future reunions and grandchildren. Now it is painfully all over, and where is the in-law?

To make the pains worse, these elder parents and grandparents know this kind of lifestyle is a sin against their God. That hurts very deeply!

And to add pain to hurt, their own pastors are now giving counsel and advice contrary to what they themselves taught their own children. Some pastors are encouraging and performing marriages to previously married persons, even though fathers object because of deep held convictions. Pastors are going against the teachings of the Word of God.

Broken vows tear apart individuals, marriages, families, churches, and their leaders. It is little wonder that God says, "I hate divorce." Note that message Malachi delivered from God. "Have we not all one Father? Did not one God create us? Why do we profane the covenant of our fathers by breaking faith with one another? Judah has broken faith. A detestable thing has been committed in Israel and in Jerusalem: Judah has desecrated the sanctuary the Lord loves, by marrying the daughter of a foreign god. As for the man who does this, whoever he may be, may the Lord cut him off from the tents of Jacob—even though he brings offerings to the Lord Almighty. Another thing you do: You flood the Lord's altar with tears. You weep and wail because he no longer pays attention to your offerings or accepts them with pleasure from your hands. You ask, Why? It is because the Lord is acting as the witness between you and the wife of your youth, because you have broken faith with her, though she is your partner, the wife of your marriage covenant. Has not the Lord made them one? In flesh and spirit they are his. And why one? Because he was seeking godly offspring. So guard yourself in your spirit, and do not break faith with the wife of your youth. I hate divorce, says the Lord God of Israel, and I hate a man's covering himself with violence as well as with his garment, says the Lord Almighty." [67]

Do you know what is so sad and revolting about this national sin that is bringing a curse upon us; this sin that is so obnoxious and hated by God? Much of the Church is being influenced by what is culturally accepted, rather than being grounded on the Word of God. If it becomes the accepted norm within the community, it becomes accepted in the Church. Now divorce and remarriage are becoming the accepted commonplace practice inside the fellowship of the Church. Since God says, "I hate divorce," He should be the final word and authority for Bible believing Churches.

Broken vows in marriages are a sin against the children, a sin against the partners, and an obnoxious offense and sin against God. I believe God's desperate call to the Church and her leaders is to repent of this sin and cleanse our ungodly way of life. (See 2 Chronicles 7:14 for the solution.)

[63] David A. Seamands *"Putting Away Childish Things"* Victor Books, Wheaton, IL.
[64] Jim Conway *"Men in Mid-Life Crisis"* David C. Cook, Elgin, IL.
[65] *The Washington Post* June 25, 1986.
[66] *Journal of Tears,* Elizabeth Lapp, Christian Light Publications.
[67] Malachi 2:10-16.

Questions for Discussion

1. How important is it that one have his/her mind made up about commitments before a temptation to break them presents itself?
2. What are the effects of broken vows on children, spouses, the church, the community?
3. What about vows of the type made by Jepthah (Judges 11)?
4. Why does God hate divorce (Malachi 2:10-16)?
5. Why do you think so many Christians seem to be taking their cues from the WORLD instead of the WORD?
6. Describe the "snowball" effect that occurs when people begin to "ease up" on their commitments.

FIVE

When Vows Aren't Kept in the Church

BRIAN AND HIS WIFE Judy have moved into the community. They have both made commitments to Jesus Christ, and wanted to find a church to attend and become part of the fellowship. They attended the "Local Bible Church," and became members. This Church has a written position as part of their living for Jesus that states members shall at no time drink alcoholic beverages. Brian and Judy promised their loyalty to Christ and to the congregation when they became members. Such a promise means they will not drink alcoholic beverages. This promise is to guide them through situations where they must decide whether to drink or abstain. If everyone in the Church is true to their commitments, this Church will not become a "drinking Church." However, as Brian attends business meetings and weddings, he becomes aware that certain people in the church do drink on "special" occasions. The deacon's daughter is marrying a gentleman from another denomination where the family is accustomed to serving "special drink" at weddings. And surely they wouldn't want to offend these people, so in this case the promise to the Church can be broken.

At the business meeting the following week he notices that one of the Sunday school teachers from the Church did not pass up the "spirits" that were offered. Brian is confused. He raises some questions, and is told that the "rule" is on the books, but isn't really being upheld. Since Brian has had a drinking appetite before becoming a Christian, he takes advantage of the advice and enjoys his favorite drink on many occasions. Therefore, the "Local Bible Church" has become a church where its members now drink alcoholic beverages.

Who is responsible? Who brought such a curse upon the Church? The people who broke their commitment to the Church! The people who decided to do what was right in their own eyes! Those who broke their commitments!

Any organization must have some understanding of how it will function and carry on its operation. When there is a standard of conduct and policy to follow it gives stability and strength to the organization. What time you are to be at work is generally an understood policy. That becomes your reference point to tell if you are late. If your local drug store has a sign in the front window that says they open at 9:00 o'clock, then you expect it to be open at 9:00 a.m. If a customer is at the door at 9:02 a.m. and finds it is still locked, a glance at the watch declares the manager is late. What would you think if the manager was a half hour late every day? You would consider that a poor way to do business!

The Church of Jesus Christ is not excluded from having a functional understanding and a standard of conduct to live by in daily life.

To become a member of a church, a vow or commitment of loyalty is generally made to God and to the Church. When persons are received into the membership, it is understood that they will uphold and express in their daily lives the understood positions of the congregation. For example, in the Mennonite Church a commitment and vow is made by the person receiving baptism and membership into the Church. The applicant vows to God and the

Church to be faithful until death. In some cases the applicant makes this vow while kneeling before God and the Church.

The applicant for baptism is asked, "Are you truly sorry for your past sins and are you willing to renounce Satan, the world, and all the works of darkness and your own carnal will and sinful desires?" The vow and the promise is, "I am." The applicant is then asked, "Do you promise by the grace of God and the aid of His Holy Spirit, to submit yourself to Christ and His Word, and faithfully to abide in the same until death?" The vow and the promise is, "I do." [68] Is that vow to be kept? Doesn't that vow mean loyalty and obedience to the Church?

People who are received into the membership of the Church from other denominations make similar vows: "Do you confess that you are of the same mind with us in the doctrine and rules of the Church; and do you promise to remain faithful and obedient in the same until death?" [69] What does it mean to say "I do"? Does it mean doing what seems right in your own eyes? Or does it mean you will be loyal and dedicated to the position of the Church you promised to be faithful to?

What about the minister who promises to "preach only the Word of God in its purity, defending its doctrines as understood by the Mennonite Church?" That's a vow! That's a promise! Is it to be kept, or is it simply a procedure to go through to get into the ministry? Is he then free to teach whatever new doctrine is right in his own eyes? Or does he have a vow of loyalty to uphold and a church position to teach? Yes, these vows are important! Yes, these vows are to be kept! To not open the drug store on time is bad business. To not keep your Christian vows is disloyalty. These vows are for stability and to hold the Church on course with the Scripture and to keep the Church from drifting into apostasy. Keeping of these vows is to protect the Church from being deceived by the forces of Satan in the last days. Making and keeping vows are to hold us faithful until death or until Jesus comes again.

When Vows Aren't Kept

Once upon a time—as stories go—when people became members of the Church, they also conformed to the doctrine and practice of the congregation where they became members. The Mennonite Church, along with several other denominations, has traditionally understood the Scripture to teach that Christian women ought to be veiled. In a certain Mennonite conference there was an understood "Statement of Christian Doctrine and Rules and Discipline of the Mennonite Church." It states; "According to the teaching of 1 Corinthians 11:1-16; 1 Timothy 2:12; and 1 Corinthians 14:34-38; the Christian woman shall wear an appropriate veiling at all times for worship, prayer, teaching, and for a constant testimony that she accepts her position as a Christian woman. When sisters of the Church give evidence of a decline in spirituality and devotion to these principles, the ministry should admonish such members who willfully disregard the proper observance of this ordinance as specified by the Conference.

"The covering shall be of a two-piece type of sufficient size to adequately cover the head. The hair shall not be cut.

"To avoid the changing suits of apparel which are so common in the world today gives credence to uniformity in the Church. Church regulations are a solution to the problem of worldliness in attire.

"For the brethren: other items of dress are not to be of the sport type."

Today, the lifestyle of many members of this conference shows no outward obedience to these scriptural teachings.

I recall an interesting experience I had in Washington D.C. years ago at one of the museums. I met some people who told me they were Mennonites. When I meet folks from the Anabaptist family, I usually like to learn more about their roots, and what conference and congregation they are with. To my surprise, these folks were members of this particular conference. I probably raised my eyebrows about two notches and thought, "Oh, really." I would not have known these church members, whom I assumed made vows to the Church, from any of the hell-bound worldly, pleasure seeking crowd of the broad way.

What happened that this Church changed? Did the Bishops meet to seek guidance from God and His Word? Were they praying and fasting and God delivered a message to them that said, "I didn't really mean for you to take My Word so literally?" Were the leaders searching the Scriptures and discovered that God doesn't really want His people to live true, holy lives that are separated from the practices of the world? Did they discover that God's Word says in the age of computers Christian women may cut their hair and conform to the culture of the unsaved world around them? I don't think so!

From my observations, it happened by the "each doing what is right in her own eyes" principle.

It probably went something like this: "The Bishops are too narrow-minded and strict. I don't have convictions to wear the head covering to work and to town. I don't like to be seen in town with it on." So the members started going to work and shopping without their veilings. Soon others followed. The Bishops discouraged this violation of commitment, but each did what was right in her own eyes, regardless of their vow of obedience.

Then they didn't bother with "it" for family devotions. God didn't punish them for it, and they could pray anyway. Since they didn't need "it" to pray at home, it wasn't important for social activities at church. And no one was excommunicated for not wearing it.

Soon it wasn't important for the Sunday evening service, since they were "just having a film."

The Sunday morning worship became the next victim of violations. Therefore, in this conference there are congregations where this practice is all but lost. Who is responsible? Who did not keep their vow?

The 1963 Mennonite Confession of Faith, Article 14 states, "The New Testament symbols of man's headship are to be his short hair and uncovered head while praying or prophesying; and the symbols of woman's role are her long hair and her veiled head."

It further states in Article 16, "We believe their adornment should be a beauty of spirit, expressed in attire that is modest, economical, simple, and becoming to those professing Christian faith."

A Sunday morning visit to many Mennonite congregations reveals very clearly somebody isn't keeping the commitments to the Church. Sisters are unveiled and bareheaded, with short hair and the latest styles. The Biblical symbol referred to in Article 14 has been replaced with jewelry and make-up. The sign of Scriptural obedience has been exchanged for the symbols of this ungodly, faddish American culture. Instead of the New Testament symbol for the Christian woman, she is now covered with symbols suggested by the money hungry fashion designers from the kingdom of this evil world.

The denomination that penned this 1963 Confession of Faith now has members whose lifestyles are contrary to the stated postion of the Church. The husband, the man, sits beside his wife for worship. Instead of the long hair and veiled head on the woman, as the Confession states, she has shortly cut hair, and unveiled head, and is wearing jewelry like the culture around her. Her husband sits beside her with longer hair than hers. This, it seems to me, is a result of willful disobedience to the Confession held by the Church.

Remember the story about Jesse, the plumber? He broke promise after promise. A promise of coming the next day, or on Friday, or next week. The Church writes her statements of faith and practice. People violate and discontinue observing what is written. Like Jesse, the plumber, the Church is forced to rewrite and adjust her theology and faith statements to line up with how her members live. Thus, we have the Church periodically adjusting her theology to fit their lifestyle.

Is this the "Spirit led" church life? I do not think so. This is operating by default. This is failure to do what is required. It is the principle of "everyone does what is right in his own eyes." This is what is taking the Church down the road on Apostasy Freeway, departing from Faith City to the Land of Deception. God warned Israel and told them, "You are not to do as we do here today, everyone as he sees fit, since you have not yet reached your resting place and the inheritance the Lord your God is giving you. But you are to cross the Jordan and settle in the land the Lord your God is giving you as an inheritance, and he will give you rest from all your enemies among you so that you will live in safety. Then to the place the Lord your God will choose as a dwelling for his Name—there you are to bring everything I command you . . . and all the possessions you have vowed to the Lord." (See Deuteronomy 13:8-11.)

God had this message for Israel; do not do just what suits you, you haven't reached your promised land yet. Stick together, serve me, and keep your vows! The Church is in the age of change. The ways of the world around us are changing very rapidly. This tends to leave society unstable and insecure. I believe God's message to Israel is also His will for the Church traveling through a wicked and immoral world; don't do just what seems right in your own eyes; you haven't reached heaven yet. Stick together, serve me, and keep your vows!

Let's look closer at who started the sin of vow breaking in the Church. Was it today's youth? No! Today's young adults? No! today's middle aged parents with grown children and little grandchildren? I think that is where it began! At least, that is when open defiance become obvious. It was my generation and older who openly began the church vow breaking process. They—we—began doing what seemed acceptable and right in our own eyes. We set a pattern for our children!

Now, who is breaking their marriage vows and doing what seems good to themselves? Who are the people that are openly divorcing and remarrying? Today's young adults? Today's young people? Yes on both questions! Do you see any connection in the behavior pattern? To me, the connection is very obvious!

In my younger years, I saw and heard disrespect for the Church, its position, and its leaders. I observed leaders doing what they wanted regardless of the Church's stated position or their vow of ordination. This principle picked up momentum like a run-away truck. It *forced* change of church polity. Today, divorce and remarriage are becoming the accepted lifestyle within the Church. Why? Because someone within the Church started breaking his vows. People started doing what was right in their own eyes. They began following the "me" principle instead of the "we" principle.

If Mom and Dad didn't keep their vows to the Church, why should their children keep marriage vows? The vow breaking principle goes on, one generation to another. Since vows to the Church are not considered binding, they are no longer an issue. Therefore, the vow breaking principle is already set in place when the children make their marriage vows.

This word to parents: Your attitudes toward the authority of the Church, the leaders, their personality and leadership style will be picked up by your children. If your attitude has any hint of rebellion or resentment, it will be picked up by your children and nurture their already rebellious attitude they inherited the day they were born. You cannot harbor bitterness, resentment, or inward rebellion without passing it on to your children. To boast about "getting away with something or putting one over the pastor" communicates that disloyalty is acceptable if you don' get caught. Vow breakers and wrong attitudes reap bitter consequences.

The Christian Booksellers Convention was held in Washington, D.C. several years ago. I went to browse the display area to learn about new books, and meet the authors. As I was approaching the Convention Hall, a large white limousine drove up to the entrance. I was curious who the important government official might be that was being chauffeured to this meeting. To my amazement, Tammy Faye Bakker was the person who had this extravagant service. Her indulgence in make-up and jewelry in no way reflected the lifestyle of a disciple of Christ who was a member of a denomination that is "holding up Bible standards against all forms of worldliness." The denomination to which she then belonged urges "all believers to 'Love not the world, neither the things that are in the world.' " [70]

Jim and Tammy Bakker have become known for their personal wealth and excessively lavish indulgence in material things. They went far beyond the Biblical admonition of being content with food and raiment. (See 1 Timothy 6:8.) While much of the world was without food, their dog was pampered in an air-conditioned dog house.

Their stylish, high-society living became public knowledge with a sex scandal that involved Jim Bakker. Shame and disgrace swept over the world-wide body of Christ.

The Church burned with shame and embarrassment. It brought disgrace to Christ's body and the Assemblies of God [Church] to which the Bakkers belonged. Was there any connection between this case and keeping commitments?

The Assemblies of God bylaws state: "In its teaching regarding worldliness, the Scripture warns against participation in activity which defiles the body, or corrupts the mind and the spirit; the inordinate love of or preoccupation with pleasures, position, or possessions, which lead to their misuse; manifestation of extreme behavior, unbecoming speech, or inappropriate appearance; any fascination or association which lessens one's affections for spiritual things."[71]

It is obvious to see that both the teaching of Scripture and the written by-laws of the Assemblies of God were violated. Loyalty to their own denomination's standard would have prevented a disgrace to the Name of Jesus, and a shaming of the Assemblies of God.

Following close to this case came yet another blow to the body of Christ when a hell-fire preacher, Jimmy Swaggart, confessed to moral failure.

"Once again the hapless Assemblies of God found itself caught in an unhappy wrangle involving one of its leading evangelists. Tarred for the second time with the brush of a steamy sex scandal, its reputation as a conservative, missions-minded denomination of high integrity has been tarnished in everything from Newsweek to Nightline.

"In order to keep their credentials, all Assemblies pastors must sign an annual agreement binding them to the standards of the constitution of the denomination." [72]

From the information I have available, Swaggart would have saved himself, the body of Christ, and his denomination much shame and embarrassment if he would have remained true to his agreement, and the denomination's warning "against . . . any fascination or association which lessens one's affection for spiritual things."

Rather than submit to the discipline of the authority structure God had placed over them, Bakker and Swaggart chose to leave the Assemblies of God.

What happens when vows to God and the Church aren't faithfully kept? It rapidly moves the Church from loyalty and faithfulness to apostasy and disobedience to God and His written Word.

---

[68] Confession of Faith and Minister's Manual, Mennonite Publishing House, 9th Edition, Scottdale, PA.

[69] *Ibid.*

[70] By-law, *The General Council of the Assemblies of God,* Sect. 6, Worldliness, p. 130.

[71] *Ibid.,* pp. 130-131.

[72] *Christianity Today,* May 13, 1988, p. 936.

Questions for Discussion

1. Why is it necessary for a church to expect its members to make commitments and then live up to them?

2. Should a change in the world's culture and traditions in any way affect the Christian's commitments?

3. If a church does see a valid need to make changes in the commitments it asks of its members, how should it go about it?

4. Review some of the vows you have made in the past. What is your faithful compliance record?

5. What do you think started the cycle of vow breaking that has come upon so many churches in recent years?

6. What are the personal effects upon the lives of individuals who break their vows?

SIX

Looking Ahead Through Commitment

"THEREFORE, BROTHERS, since we have confidence to enter the Most Holy Place by the blood of Jesus, by a new and living way opened for us through the curtain, that is, his body, and since we have a great priest over the house of God, let us draw near to God with a sincere heart in full assurance of faith, having our hearts sprinkled to cleanse us from a guilty conscience and having our bodies washed with pure water. Let us hold unswervingly to the hope we profess, for he who promised is faithful. And let us consider how we may spur one another on toward love and good deeds. Let us not give up meeting together, as some are in the habit of doing, but let us encourage one another —and all the more as you see the Day approaching." [73]

This passage of Scripture emphasizes the need for believers to be close and committed to each other. It teaches that we need each other.

"So I made up my mind that I would not make another painful visit to you. For if I grieve you, who is left to make me glad but you whom I have grieved? I wrote as I did so that when I came I should not be distressed by those who ought to make me rejoice. I had confidence in all of you, that you would all share my joy." [74]

We are the Epistles the unbeliever reads. What we live, others perceive to be God's will.

George Muller, who is known for his outstanding work with a home for orphans which he started in 1835, was also known for some of his wise sayings. He addressed the sin of vow breaking.

"It has often been mentioned to me, in various places, that brethren in business do not sufficiently fulfill the keeping of promises, and I cannot therefore but entreat all who love our Lord Jesus, and who are engaged in a trade or business, to seek for His sake not to make any promises, except they have every reason to believe they shall be able to fulfill them, and therefore carefully to weigh all the circumstances before making any engagement, lest they should fail in its accomplishment. It is even in these little ordinary affairs of life that we may either bring much honor or dishonor to the Lord: and these are the things every unbeliever can take notice of. Why should it be so often said, and sometimes with a measure of ground, or even much ground: 'Believers are bad servants, bad tradesmen, bad masters'? Surely it ought not to be true that we, who have power with God to obtain by prayer and faith all needful grace, wisdom, and skill, should be bad servants, bad tradesmen, bad masters." [75]

George Muller saw vow breaking as a problem in his day. He addressed the problem with the reminder that it dishonors and degrades the name of our Lord. For the sake of Jesus Christ and His great Name, believers should be true and trustworthy. We either bring honor or dishonor to our Lord by the way we keep our promises. We have the power of the Holy Spirit, the written Word of God, the fellowship of prayer, and the supporting Church to be the best promise keepers in the world. Muller saw that being unfaithful servants and not keeping promises was a disgrace, and dishonored the Lord Himself.

It's a Principle

Keeping promises is scriptural. It is wrong to break promises at any point, and violate Scripture. If you have made a contract, or promise, or work contract, you are under obligation to fulfill it in a satisfactory manner. If you told your widowed neighbor you would replace her window, then do it. As long as it is not fixed, it is an unfulfilled promise.

The believer should honor his Lord by keeping promises in all areas of life. His promises to Christ and the Church, to his wife, to his children, in business and in social events are all binding. If you are mediocre in keeping promises in any area of life, you are not a faithful vow keeper, and likely are poor in keeping promises in all areas of life. If you promise your son something to get him "off your back," and then do not fulfill it, you are a vow breaker.

Breaking vows has brought an ugly stigma on God's people, the Church. It is a disgrace and dishonor to God when you cannot have complete confidence in the honesty and integrity of God's people. The confidence and support of a congregation is shattered and the flock is scattered when they realize their pastor is violating his vows of ordination. Keeping promises and vows is closely associated with being a person of honesty, integrity, truthfulness, and trustworthiness. To not keep your promises strips away all of these good titles from your name, and from the name of Christ.

Be a Pattern

Looking ahead, we need reliable patterns. We need people who are living designs and models of promise keepers. Would your life make a good pattern of loyalty to your commitments? Would you make a good pattern for

the children and teen-agers to copy? Would it be upbuild-
ing to take your pattern to mold your your children and
grandchildren? Would you make a pattern of an unmistak-
ably staunch disciple of Jesus Christ? What would your
Church and community be like if everyone used you for a
pattern?

The Scripture calls believers to be examples and
patterns of what a disciple of Jesus Christ ought to be. "Be
an example (pattern) for the believers in speech, in conduct, in love, in faith, in purity." [76]

One of the most pathetic and sad commentaries about
some of our "peace Churches" is the example of the
witness. While they are calling nations to abandon warfare,
and demonstrate against government action and policy,
they fail to maintain peace and commitment in marriages.
They are calling on two nations to do what two individuals
are not willing to do. The "peace Churches" should be the
prime example of vow keeping and peace in marriages.

One of America's influential preachers is a member of
the Southern Baptist denomination. "Almost all Southern
Baptist Churches use the traditional Baptist covenant in
which members agree not to use or sell intoxicating drinks
as a beverage." In spite of this covenant, this preacher
admits that "he and his wife drink alcoholic wine, since he
can find nothing in the Bible to forbid it."[77]

"For even hereunto were ye called: because Christ also
suffered for us, leaving us an example, that ye should
follow in his steps." [78]

Be a Preserver

Looking ahead, we must begin to be preservers. Jesus
said, "Ye are the salt of the earth: but if the salt have lost his
savour, wherewith shall it be salted? It is thenceforth good
for nothing, but to be cast out, and to be trodden under foot
of men. Ye are the light of the world. A city that is set on an

hill cannot be hid. Neither do men light a candle, and put it under a bushel, but on a candlestick; and it giveth light unto all that are in the house. Let your light so shine before men, that they may see your good works, and glorify your Father which is in heaven." [79]

You, the believer, are the salt of the earth, the preserver of biblical principles. If you do not express a pattern of honesty, truthfulness, and keeping of vows in your daily life, who will? Don't count on the politicians to do it. Don't depend on government leaders to preserve it. We become disturbed when politicians make promises in their campaigns, and then do not keep them. The believer is to be the preserver, the salt, the light, and the pattern; not the unbelieving politician, or the ungodly world.

During Jesus' earthly life, the people faced a similar problem. They could not trust the religious leaders. The words of the leaders and their conduct did not gain the trust of the people. Therefore, they attempted to strengthen their words by swearing. Jesus addressed this problem in His Sermon on the Mount.

"Again, ye have heard that it hath been said by them of old time, Thou shalt not forswear theyself, but shalt perform unto the Lord thine oaths: But I say unto you, Swear not at all; neither by heaven; for it is God's throne: Nor by the earth; for it is his footstool: neither by Jerusalem; for it is the city of the great King. Neither shalt thou swear by thy head, because thou canst not make one hair white or black. But let your communication be, Yea, yea; Nay, nay: for whatsoever is more than these cometh of evil." [80]

Modern society today has the same problem. People swear they are telling the truth. they declare "God be my witness," and "I cross my heart and hope to die." "May God strike me dead if I am not telling the truth." However, this does not establish trustworthiness. People are disappointed and hurt when promises are not kept. Emphasizing your truthfulness by making promises or declaring you are telling the truth this time does not establish you as a person of integrity and honesty. It does not make you believable and worthy of trust.

God wants the believers to be persons whose words can be trusted and believed. He wants them to be trustworthy. God expects His people to be the preservers of keeping their promises to Him, to His Church, and to each other. Who can trust a minister to interpret the Scripture if he has not kept his ordination vow? How can you trust a person who has broken a marriage promise? If believers are not the pattern in keeping these most serious vows, is there any wonder we don't trust each other?

Be Repentant

Looking ahead, the Church needs to deal with the sin of vow breaking and respond with repentance before God and the Church. In order to experience God's blessing and revival, there needs to be an atmosphere of repentant attitudes permeating the Church. The spirit of indifference and arrogance toward vow keeping hinders the work of the Spirit among God's people. God's message to the Church at Ephesus was to repent because "thou hast left thy first love." This Church was known for its hard work, its patience, and how it could not tolerate evil men who claimed to be apostles, but in reality were liars. This Church suffered for the sake of the Lord, and did not give up. There was one problem, "But this is what I have against you: you do not love me now as you did at first." [81]

What was God's solution? "Remember therefore from whence thou art fallen, and repent, and do the first works; or else I will come unto thee quickly, and will remove thy candlestick out of his place, except thou repent." [82]

What is the message for today? You have left and forsaken your first love for God. You have broken your love-vows. You have departed from your love-vows in marriage. You have fallen!

The word from God is repent! The remedy for the problem is repentance. If you are not a good pattern of keeping vows, repent!

If you have violated your marriage vows, repent!

If your actions and lifestyle have been following your "me policy" of doing what is right in your own eyes, repent!

If doing what is right in your own eyes has brought disobedience to the Scripture into the body of Christ, repent!

If you were involved in scheming "politics," pressure groups, and aligning peer pressure to gain changes and force leaders to change church policy by default, repent!

If you have violated the position of the Church, and by that violation influenced others to rebel, you need a repentant attitude that brings repentance to the Church.

Our history has some unpleasant accounts of forced policy changes brought upon the leaders and directors of institutions by groups who wanted what was right in their own eyes. Pressures were put upon God's chosen and ordained leaders to "give in" and allow disobedience to Scripture and stated positions of the Church. Collective, pressure-inspired disobedience to church positions has moved the Church more in line with the marching orders of the world system.

Have we lost our first love and respect for God, for one another, and for God's ordained leadership? Is getting our own way more important than respect and love for leadership? Is getting what we want more important than relationships? If so, God is calling us to repentance.

Does this mean there is no way to change church policy and statements of faith? No, it doesn't mean that! There is a way of change that allows God's blessings to be upon the Church. There is a way that has more safeguards than breaking vows. It is called appealing, reasoning, fasting, praying, seeking God's will under the guidance of His Word through the leaders of the Church. It can be Godly change as His people work together in the spirit of submission and repentance. We can more clearly discern God's will if we approach His presence with a repentant attitude. God is still able to work through His elected and ordained leaders in discerning how to live for Him in this sinful and adulterous generation.

Breaking the Cycle

Looking ahead, we must break the cycle. Some of our self-destructive patterns are passed from one generation to the next. Just because grandpa did it does not necessarily make it right.

Grandpa was not going to put up with some "stupid" church rule that dictated what he ought to wear, so he took it into his own hands to change it by doing as he pleased. With a tinge of boasting, he tells his grandchildren how things used to be thirty years ago, and how he was one of the first to get things changed by pressuring the leader to give into the demands of the people.

His son wasn't going to have some "stupid" rule keep him from seeing whatever movie he wanted to see at the local drive-in. So he took it in his own hands to change the matter. He even boasted to his peers about his self-ordained freedom, and what he saw at the theater.

His grandson isn't going to have some "stupid" church rule tell him when he can sleep with his girl friend, and when he can't. So he, like those before him, takes it into his own hands to change the rule.

The Scripture speaks of "visiting the iniquities of the fathers upon the children unto the third and fourth generation." [83] We become like a stuck record. The same sin repeats itself, each generation breaking whatever promise does not suit its selfish desires. Therefore, we unrelentingly pass on the sins of our fathers to the next generation. May this generation break the vow breaking cycle, and pass on the succeeding generation an example of integrity, self denial, and sacrificial living.

In the day of the Model T Ford, a car would be driven over the same roads and same ruts day after day. Finally, the ruts became so deep the car got stuck in the mud. Help was required to pull it out. Some believers are stuck in the rut of vow breaking. Help is needed to break this cycle. This cycle can be broken. We can get out of the rut. It can happen as we confess our sins to God, seek His forgiveness, and seek supporting help from our brothers and sisters in the Church. God's Spirit is greater than the spirit of this world. He will enable a believer, who chooses to be a vow keeper, to keep his vows, even while living in this sinful and adulterous generation.

Our young people stand on the threshold of the future. As they glance backwards, and then look ahead into the unknown future, they ask questions. What's the point in holding the line on morals now, if in ten years our present sins will become the accepted norm? Is it only a matter of time until we accept adultery and homosexual marriages within the membership of the Church? Since Scripture can so quickly be re-interpreted to have women ordained into the ministry, will they do the same with sex before marriage? If it is going to be an acceptable behavior in ten years, why restrain myself now? According to the lessons of history, that may be what is ahead.

Young people from the more "conservative" Churches are asking if their Churches will be like the more "liberal" Churches in ten to twenty years. If that is the case, why bother holding the line now?

So what is the Church in the future going to be like? It

depends very much on how you keep your vows to your Church today! That is where it is! If we continue to compare ourselves among ourselves, and justify our sins and Church violations because others do it, we will continue destroying the Church. If we live by the "he does it, and gets by, the preacher hasn't said anything about it, so I'll do it, too" philosophy, we will tear down whatever remaining standard is left.

Isaiah said, "Lift up a standard for the people." Why should the preacher need to say anything? Your commitment of faithfulness should hold you regardless of what others do. Jane wearing jewelry and Brian drinking alcoholic beverages do not make it right for you. This copying disobedience one from another irrespective of church vows is destroying the Church and its mission. You are to be a pattern, not a copy of a wrong pattern.

Can the cycle be broken? When the enemy comes in like a flood, can there be a standard that forces him to stop? Can the Spirit of the Lord "lift up a standard against him"? Can we stop breaking our vows and be strong and loyal? Yes, we can!

However, it must be treated as a serious sin. It must be treated and approached in a similar manner that an alcoholic faces his problems. It is a sin against God and humanity, and the offender must take drastic steps of repentance, self-discipline and determination to live victorious. The offender, as the alcoholic, needs the encouraging support of dedicated disciples of Jesus to help and encourage in the overcoming process. Some sins in the Church are more deadly than alcohol. Because the destructiveness is easier to hide, we tend to overlook them. I believe vow breaking is one of these destructive sins.

When we become new persons in Christ, we receive God's forgiveness. However, receiving God's gift of forgiveness does not of itself break all sin cycles in our life. It does not automatically break all rebellious patterns that have been followed for years. Some stubborn deep-seated sin patterns must be singled out and brought to God for changing. These sins must be treated as deadly threats to our relationship with God and with others. We must seek absolute and complete deliverance through God. I see this vow breaking cycle as one of these sins.

While I was on a Choice Books service run to one of the major chain stores, I asked permission to use their men's room. On the outside of the door was a sign, "Please no magazines, they belong on the shelf." On the inside of the door was a daily cleaning schedule with a place to check duties peformed. There was a place to check after cleaning the walls, door, sink, toilet, and floor. There was also a check list for soap, trash cans, paper towels, and tissues. This men's room ought to be in top shape! It had the proper statement of cleaning, employees were working in the store, and the sign on the front door was given by the manager. Remember, the sign on the door says, "No magazines." I opened the door, and there were three magazines lying on the floor. The walls were dirty, the door had a loose latch, the sink had other items on it, the toilet seat was broken, the mirror was spotted, the floor was unkept and trashy, and there were no paper towels. There were three partly used rolls of tissue cluttered around, but the spool was empty. There was soap and a partly filled trash can. So what is new about dirty men's rooms? Nothing—except the conspicuous sanitary rules and how they were openly violated and ignored. What does this do for the reputation of the chain store, the manager, or the employees? It appeared as though the right doctrine was on the door, but the poeple did what they felt like doing.

This men's room stirred an ugly comparison in my mind. It reminded me of people, couples, church members, and ministers who had the right signs, the right words, and made the right vows; but ignored them. Because they ignore them, it puts an ugly stigma upon their Manager, the Lord Himself. It gives the Church and the people a bad reputation. It gives the violator a poor name. This men's room reminds me of Jesse, the plumber; the man who broke his marriage vow; the heart-broken children resulting from divorce; the church members who ignore their church vows; and the preacher who overlooks the church covenant in favor of alcoholic beverages. That is the kind of cluttered Church and world we have as each does what is right in his own eyes.

We are living in the age of "everyone do your own thing," and "if it feels good, do it." I believe those who give in and follow that spirit are ushering in a departing "from the faith, giving heed to seductive spirits, and doctrines of the devil."

God is calling you to be a reliable example. He is calling you to be a consistent preserver. God is calling His Church from the air of arrogance into an atmosphere of contrition and repentance, to break the vow breaking cycle.

Looking ahead, I know this will mean a sacrifice on our part. It means we are committed to something bigger than ourselves, and that we can't do just what we feel like doing. On the other hand, as I see the next, and the next generaion following closely behind, I firmly believe it is worth making vow keeping a priority in our lives. It is worth laying aside some of our self-will for the sake of our children and grandchildren. It's worth it to be able to tell your children and grandchildren, "I promised, that is why!"

The future of the Church will be shaped by the way we keep our commitments.

[73] Hebrews 10:18-25 N.I.V.

[74] 2 Corinthians 2:1-3 N.I.V.

[75] *George Muller of Bristol,* Arthur T. Pierson, Zondervan Publications, Grand Rapids, MI 1984, p. 344.

[76] 1 Timothy 4:12b Amplified.

[77] Capitol Voice, Sept. 1, 1987.

[78] 1 Peter 2:21.

[79] Matthew 5:13-16.

[80] Matthew 5:33-37.

[81] Revelation 2:4 T.E.V.

[82] Revelation 2:5.

[83] Numbers 14:18, Exodus 34:7, 20:5.

Questions for Discussion

1. How does a broken vow dishonor the Lord?

2. It used to be said of Mennonite people that, "Their word was as good as their bond." Do you think this is still true?

3. Point out some inconsistencies between the "walk" and the "talk" of some Christians in the area of commitment keeping.

4. Do you think taking an oath helps to strengthen one's vows and promises?

5. What do you think can be done to break the present cycle of broken baptismal and marriage vows?

6. What has the reading of this book done for your views of vow making and breaking?

Distributed by Choice Books
11923 Lee Highway, Fairfax, VA 22030   (703) 830-2800

Order extra copies from:

Choice Books
11923 Lee Highway,
Fairfax, VA 22030

(703) 830-2800